PIECES OF MY LIFE

Overcoming Childhood Trauma Through Perseverance

By

Tracy Young

ISBN: 978-1-948777-10-0

Acknowledgements

My beautiful family: Everett, Everett Jr. Khristina and Todd, thank you for loving me and giving me the space to spread my wings. You all are the wind beneath my wings and my soft place to land.

I am who I am today because so many people have touched my life. Everything from a word of encouragement, tough love, compassion, understanding and belief was given to me at some point in my life, and for that I want to thank you. You have supported me throughout my journey and I will forever be grateful for you.

I cannot list everyone, but just to name a few people past or present who have made a major impact on my life:

Carrie Jones, Deborah Thomas, Kawena Cole, Lynn Hopkins, Larry Shelbourn, Marjorie Becnel, Kimble Mealancon, LaTanya Allen, Jordan Banner, Melinda Murphy, Patrise Burney, Nkem Anene, Melody Gray, Beth

Minor, Pamela Burney, Jeffery Gray, Judge Emily Stevens, Attorney Francine Davis, Carolyn Wright, Michael Roettger, Carmen Roettger, Stephanie Hillman, Donald Hillman

Dedication

This book is dedicated to little Tracy, You can rest assured that everything that you were created for and aspire to do will be accomplished. I will continue to sound the alarms, make noise and shake up the world through sharing pieces of your life. Breathe and know that great change will happen as a result of your courage and bravery.

Also to my foster sister Tanae:

Although your life was cut short by a senseless act of violence, rest assured that I have never forgotten our late-night talks in that group home. I have and will continue to share our experiences to positively impact this world. I carry you with me. I have us, you can trust me.

When you hear a person being described by the following words: suicidal, homicidal, angry, depressed, violent, delinquent, and anxious, how do you feel, and what comes to mind? When you think of an abused or neglected child, what comes to mind, and what expectations does society have for them? When you think of a product of the child welfare system (foster care), what comes to mind? What would you expect from someone who has worn all of the labels above? Would you expect them to be successful, have an amazing family, married, college educated, a motivational speaker, or someone who people look up to? If I had to guess, I would say probably not. According to studies and what is depicted in society, there isn't much one would expect from a person with such a resume.

Well, that's me all wrapped up in a bow, and I wouldn't change one second of it. My present circumstances have far exceeded the expectations for my life according to statistics.

I want to introduce you to *Pieces of My Life.* The story you are about to read describes parts of my life that I have chosen to share with you and the world. As interesting or disturbing as these parts of my life may have been, they are pieces of my life. These events have shaped me from the inside out, and through them I have learned how to move beyond my circumstances and make the best of any situation. I hope they will inspire you as well. As a result of reading this book, your mindset will shift concerning the power of resilience and what is possible when you put your mind to it. After reading this I hope you choose to never give up or stop dreaming. I hope that you are encouraged to trust and believe in yourself even if no one else does. As a result of reading this book I hope you will be inspired and know that it is possible to overcome hurt, pain, abuse and depression, failure, low self-esteem, and so much more through perseverance and determination. Lastly, I hope that you will take your power back and create the life that you desire realizing that you get to choose how you show up in the world. Although my childhood included many sad days, those sad days helped me develop into the person that I am today. I believe that these experiences have afforded me an opportunity to gain insight and appreciation for many things that would have otherwise been taken for granted. I have also come to realize that everything happens for a reason.

Who is this book for?

This book is for anyone and everyone who is navigating through this thing called life. If you have *ever* had a rough day, this is for you. This includes but is not limited to the everyday human being, victims, survivors, caregivers, social workers, teachers, law enforcement, and/or anyone else who is interested in tapping into the power of resilience and their own strength.

This book is meant to be Neosporin to heal old or new cuts in your life. Apply the lessons learned in these pages as you would Desitin, allowing them to soothe the places where life has rubbed you the wrong way.

My hope is that you are inspired and encouraged to move beyond anything because you have what it takes to make it. You will have a chance to see what possibility looks like. I am living proof that you can endure neglect and abuse and still rise like a phoenix. After all, we are not what happens to us. We are what we choose to do with the things that have happened to us

Contents

Piece 1

No More Sleep

It's dark and I am finally falling asleep, my eyes are heavy my breathing is getting deeper. Today was a long day; panhandling, changing their diapers, cooking dinner, and being punched a few times was enough. As I lay facing the wall of the couch, I can see the moonlight. I stare at the sky for a bit and just take in all its beauty. I am a little sore and very tired, but I somehow manage to look at the moon, and for a moment, escape my present worries. I finally fall asleep. Suddenly, I felt something change in the room; there is a different light and another presence in the room. I look back and there is a shadow of a person standing close. No they are not just standing close, they're standing over me. Before I worked up the courage to look, I am laying there frozen and wondering who could this large presence be in my room at this time of night? I wait a few more seconds to hear a voice or for the being to leave, but it's still there. I finally turn around and there I see a hammer in their hand. My heart is beating so fast that I can feel it pouncing through my chest, and for some reason, this does not make sense to me. Who, what, and why is someone in my room with a hammer! It starts to become clear, the body I see is familiar to me. The hand holding the hammer, I know their touch…I look up and I scream, "*Mama, what are you doing in my room!?*" She remains quiet with this blank stare. She is staring at me with this hammer in her hand and it does not make sense. It is between 2:00 and 4:00 a.m. and there is nothing to hammer. I scream again, "*Mama, why are you in my room?*" She then says with a soft but scary whisper, "*I came to check on you.*" I then scream, "*Why do you have a hammer?*" She looks at me and then turns and walks out of my room.

From that night on I never slept the same. I had already been struggling to fall asleep, but this changed it all! Needless to say, I did not sleep that night. Instead, I got up and figured out how I could rearrange my room to prevent this event from ever happening again. In my room, I had the couch I slept on, a desk, and a dresser. I configured my room to make sure I could block the door with a few quick pushes. All I had to do was push the dresser forward, then the desk behind it, and then slide the couch right behind the desk. I had an L setup that made the plan easy for me. She often asked me why I changed my room around, never realizing that it changed immediately following her entering my room in the middle of the night with a hammer.

We never talked about that night; it was as if it never happened. I chose not to bring it up as I wasn't up for her explanation. The fear that I felt that night when she entered my room was enough for me. The feeling that she brought when she entered my room was not up for discussion or explaining away. I can only imagine what would have happened to me if I had not turned around when I did.

There were many days following that night that the arrangement of my room saved me a few punches or kicks to the body. I stayed on alert as you could never really tell when she was going to find a reason to use you as her punching bag. There were times when a simple question about going outside or telling her that I needed something would ignite her fire. She was quick on her feet, running towards you like a bull after a red flag. I studied her and I learned to watch her body language and take off running up the stairs if she positioned her body a certain way. The times I was slow or distracted, she would snatch me by my hair, slap and punch me, often reprimanding me about interrupting her while she was watching her "stories" (*Young and the Restless, Days of our Lives, or Another World*).

I would leap up the stairs, skipping a stair or two in order to make it to my room in time to barricade myself inside. Sometimes she would pound on the door and try to push her way in, all while hurling threats about how bad she was going to "fuck you up" once she got in. At times she would pound and try to push her way in for about ten minutes. Then she'd try to bait me out of the room. She would change her tone and began to tell me how she wasn't going to hit me if I just opened the door. One time, in particular, she said "mama sorry". For her this was rare, as she rarely said she was sorry.

When I heard her say she was sorry I felt like the battle was over. I was happy to hear those words because she was big on saying she apologized but was not sorry. She explained that sorry meant you regret what you did, while apologies were just for the other person's feelings. After hearing those sweet words I slowly moved the furniture out of the way. I dried my tears, went to the door, and opened it. I was expecting a hug or for us to talk about the situation. Nope. As soon as the door opened I was greeted by her hand across my face. I fell to my knees crying and wondering how I could be so dumb. While I was settling things in my head I could hear her voice telling me how stupid I was to open the door, and how she would hurt me worse if I tried this again with her. Needless to say, this happened multiple times. I would sit up all night waiting for her to regain her strength and come back to beat on the door and hurl verbal insults through it. It took me opening the door multiple times before I realized that she was not going to change, and if something was going to be different, I would have to be the one to change, and I did. Once I figured this out, I never opened the door again.

During times that I was experiencing verbal and physical abuse at the hands of my mother, I found myself confused and in a constant state of devastation due to what was happening and being said to me. She was my mother and I worked hard to make her happy. I tried hard; I would brush her hair, scratch her head, scratch her back for hours, just hoping that she could see that I loved her and remind her that she loved me too. Sometimes it just felt like she hated me and didn't want my love. I couldn't give up and I could not understand what was so wrong with me and why she could not *see* me. I did everything I could to prove I was in her corner, but nothing seemed to matter. She didn't want me and clearly could not *see* me.

I was 12 or 13 when these events took place, and I can remember that I was fearful and felt helpless. Although I did not know what would possess my mother to enter my room with a hammer, deep inside I wondered what I had done to deserve this. All I know is that I wanted to know what was so bad about me, and what I needed to do to change it.

Notes

Piece 2

Unshaken

One morning while in elementary school I arrived at school like any other day. I joined the line to get breakfast. Waited in the long line as usual with kids screaming, laughing, and playing. I was hungry, so there was no time for playing for me right then. I finally reached the front of the counter and grabbed my tray to enter the next part of the line where we get the juice, milk, coffee, cake, or cereal. I was almost near the lady that takes the meal ticket when the unexpected happened. The laughter heard a few minutes ago had now turned to screams. It was chaos! The earth was shaking and people were running and crying. I heard adult voices telling us to get under the table, but I couldn't move.... I was stuck, petrified, and I could not stop crying. A teacher got close enough to me and yelled loud enough to shake me out of it. It seemed like that moment lasted forever.

When it was all over, all I could hear were kids crying. Crying because they didn't know what had just happened to them. I looked at the teachers and school administrators and they too were frightened. They did the best they could to gather all of the kids and stay calm. Some kids had cuts and scrapes, and some of the staff from the cafeteria area looked hurt as well. While I was crying I began to panic…Is my Mama okay?! Did the earthquake get her?! If she is okay, is she on her way to pick me up? My mind riddled with thoughts about her and my siblings made my anxiousness kick into overdrive. The school handled things very well, as they gathered us in the auditorium to help us calm down and wait for our parents. Some kids were crying uncontrollably while others appeared in shock. I have always been a crier, so the tears kept coming.

After sitting in the auditorium for about 30 minutes the parents started pouring in to get their babies. Looking at the faces of the kids when their mom or dad arrived was priceless. You know the feeling you get when something bad happens but your parents or loved ones show up? I witnessed faces of pure relief knowing that everything was going to be okay. There were a few aftershocks during the day, and every time one happened the loud cries started back up. Every time the doors opened, we had to wait to hear the name of the student who was going home, and anxiously I was hoping they would call my name. It started out with, let's say 300 kids, and by the afternoon it looked like half of them had been picked up. But not me. My mind raced constantly thinking: what happened to my mama? Did the ground crack like it did here, but maybe bigger and her car fell in? Is she dead? Is she hurt?! I cried. I cried thinking about how afraid she might be right now if she is hurt and cannot get to me. I prayed that she was safe and that if her car was in a crack, someone would help her. I kept trying to tell myself that the next time the door opened my mom was going to be there to get me.

The door opened once, but it wasn't for me. It opened again, but it wasn't for me. The door opened over and over again, yet not for me. I kept telling myself: next time it opens, it's going to be for me. They brought us lunch, and still the door does not open for me. I was then wondering how much longer I could cry, because I had been crying all day to the point that my head hurt and my stomach muscles hurt from being tightened every time the door opened. I wanted to give up, but I couldn't. I kept watching the kids leave, and I saw the look of relief on their parents' faces, so why isn't my mom here yet to get me? This just didn't make sense, she loves me, she knows I cry easily, she knows how scared I get, and she knows how safe I feel when she is around. She knows…doesn't she? Before the school day ended most of the kids were gone. There were a few of us left in the room, maybe 20 to 40, but I didn't care. I wanted to be one of the kids that got to go home. I wanted to be one of the kids who had parents frantically rushing in to get their babies, get their babies because they know that they make everything better.

The bell rang for the school day to end, and we were all free to leave the auditorium. A part of me was fearful to leave, as I was thinking that they may come and tell me she fell into a crack and is dead or hurt. I took my time gathering my belongings and going outside. I stepped outside and, due to most of the kids already being gone, the parking lot was clear. You could see all the cars of the parents there to pick up their children. She wasn't here! My mind raced, because now I think I know she is hurt or dead, because she is not here. The tears started again, and I could not keep it together. I waited with one of my siblings for what seemed like an eternity, and she finally turned the corner. She was okay. She had on her usual zip-up robe and her hair was tied back in one of her bandanas. When I got in I was anxious to find out what happened to her; surely there was a reasonable explanation as to why she didn't come get me. After saying hello, I waited a second, trying to find the words to ask her my burning question without getting hit.

I mustered up the voice and I say, "*M*ama, we had an earthquake at school today." I think I was holding my breath hoping the earthquake had only happened at my school. Everything in me wanted this to be true. She then replied, "*Yeah I know.*" I then asked her if the streets were cracked by our house, "*No,*" she replied. I then asked her if she felt it and she replied, "*Yes.*" I asked her if she was scared and she said, "*Naw, I was in my bed when it happened. I turned over and went back to sleep when it was done. It was nothing like the earthquake in 1971. DEVASTATION!*" I sat there stunned and in disbelief that this was her response. I was broken! It was as if the world stopped. My heart was crushed by her response and her inability to connect the dots. All I could think about was how many parents rushed to the aid of their children following the earthquake and this played in my head over and over. Prior to this event we had only practiced earthquake drills. Surely the parents of elementary school kids knew that this was their children's first experience in an earthquake. But clearly to my mother it was no big deal! Maybe she thought I was okay, so I wanted to make sure she knew that I wasn't. *"Mama I was scared, I was crying all day, and I wanted you to come get me."* She looked at me through the rearview mirror and said, *"Come get you for what, the earthquake was over."* I repeated how scared I was and how I wanted her to come get me, but she kept driving.

Although the conversation ended between us, my thoughts kept going. I couldn't understand how she could be this way. I started thinking about all the tears I cried and the pain I felt just thinking about her and wondering if she was okay, and all the while she didn't think about me at all. Like she said, she turned over and went back to sleep! I felt unloved and unimportant. My poor mind was on overload, constantly replaying the events of the day. Constantly showing me how other moms and dads showed up for their children, and mine did not. I wondered if their parents loved them in a different way, and if they were just as scared as their children.

Even from this young age I had feelings that consumed me. I constantly thought about how people felt and was concerned about the well-being of everyone I loved.

✦✦✦

While I wanted more from my mother and was initially disappointed and upset about her lack of concern for me following the earthquake, I quickly put the negative thoughts out of my head. My love for her was stronger than the disappointment, being devalued, and the feelings of abandonment and dismissal I felt following the earthquake. I struggled mentally with settling this in my mind, because my mind said that she should have been there and that I should be mad at her, but my heart said otherwise. My heart wanted love, and it wanted it from her. I swallowed my feelings, explained them away, and told myself that it was no big deal. I still marveled at her and wanted her approval for everything, just as most children do.

When I became a mother, I was hypersensitive. I am sure this was partially because I was a mom and a lot of moms are overprotective...over everything. But there was always something about when my children were at school and something happened in the community or they were sick. I could not leave them there out of fear that they would have a similar experience to the one I had that day the earthquake hit. I feel like that experience helped me become more sensitive to the needs of others, but it also left me in a place where I could not relax. I was always on edge when it came to my children. Over the years I learned how to calm my nerves, yet I was unable to fully conquer this situation of being hypersensitive and overprotective of my children because there was always something in the back of my head reminding me that they may need me, and if I am not there, they may think I don't care.

On a lighter note, my mom had this fun side to her, one that used to make up for all the bad. There were times when she would play card games with me and let me drink some of her RC Cola. She loved soda! There were even times when my siblings would be sleep and she would allow me to watch TV with her. I used to try really hard to fall asleep fast, with hopes that I would wake up in the middle of the night and she would let me join her in the living room. This didn't always work, as sometimes I think she caught on to the fact that I would drink water right before bed and just happen to wake up around the same time, telling her I couldn't sleep. Many times she would say, *"Go pray and go back to sleep."* Those nights I just walked right back into the room and jumped into bed and hope that next time I would be able to join her.

Notes

TOPIC:

Piece 3

Spotlights on You

I t's a sunny day outside, you can hear the kids in the neighborhood running, laughing and playing with each other. Inside my house it was dark and dim, and gloom filled the air because she is not happy today. I stay out of her sight unless called because today I am hoping to soak up the happy noise outside and drown out the discomfort within. I hear my name being called once, and then there is about a ten second break before I hear it again. I get my voice together to answer, but that must be taking too long because I then hear *"itch you don't hear me fucking calling you?!"* Immediately my voice gears up and I yell downstairs, *"Yes mama, here I come."* I take a deep breath and breathe in a little bit of the happiness from the outside kids. I come downstairs to see what she wants. She is sitting there on the couch, butt naked as usual. The skin between her eyebrows is crinkled like she is in deep thought and pissed. There's a cigarette in her hand and some soda in a cup in front of her. She motions me with her hand for me to have a seat. I sit down. One minute and then two pass by, and she has not said a word, just staring at me as if she is sizing me up. As I wait, I am looking at her with a respectful look, but inside I too am sizing her up to make sure I am ready to run if she jumps at me to hit me. False alarm because she breaks a small smile while we are in the third minute of watching each other, and she says, *"The kids need some diapers and juice."* I know this means there is a part she wants me to play, so I continue to wait for her to finish. *"I need you to stand outside and ask for a few dollars so we can get them some diapers and juice."* Fuck, I think in my head. My stomach sank! Oh no, everyone is outside. I look at the clock and it's practically evening time, so the spotlight will be on me, and I don't want to do it. Sweating a little and feeling like I may have to throw up, my mind is racing.

I'm thinking: my peers from school are some of the kids outside playing and having a good time. No way did I want to be embarrassed by begging for money from their parents. I don't want to be seen in the daylight hours begging because there would be no way for me to deny that it was me. I am panicking on the inside so I think fast and I tell her that it's too hot outside and that I think there are a few more diapers upstairs. She then tells me that now is the best time. She goes on to say that people are coming home from work or going out and they will be willing to help me. I guess she has it all figured out! She doesn't get it! She does not take into consideration the impact this will have on me. So I don't really have a choice, but I am sad and pissed all at the same time. I tell her that I don't know how to ask for money, and I try to come up with other reasons why I shouldn't do it. She said it wasn't too hot, wasn't too early, and it wasn't my choice. She then began to tell me that if they don't have diapers and juice it would be because I was being selfish. She knew how I was, there was nothing I wouldn't do for them, and she knew I didn't like being the cause of someone going without. She knew just how to manipulate me and play with my head.

I took my time putting on my clothes, and it seemed like the happiness outside was intensifying. All of a sudden it seemed like I could hear more laughter than ever before. I swore I recognized some of the voices I heard outside, and they were the voices of my peers. All I could think of was how I would never be able to live this down. The kids who already teased me about the dirty clothes I wore to school and my uncombed hair would have one more thing to talk about.

I started hoping that something would happen outside that would cause them all to stop enjoying their day and retreat to their homes, but that was only wishful thinking, as it seemed like everyone else was having a blast. After I was dressed she gave me the script and told me to hurry up and get the money. I did it! I waited for people to approach the automatic gate to leave the community and I told them that my baby siblings needed diapers and juice. Some people passed me by, while others asked, "*Where are your parents?*" I told them they weren't here, while thinking inside (yeah where the hell are the people who made these kids). I spent about an hour outside begging people for money. That hour felt like 4. I felt low begging for money, especially when I knew that my mom mismanaged the funds she received and never seemed to run low or out of soda and cigarettes the way my siblings ran out of diapers and juice and how I ran out of sanitary napkins and clean clothes to wear.

In that hour I raised about $25.00, which was enough to buy a pack of diapers and juice for the babies. I entered the apartment happy to be done with this task and because the babies would have what they needed and I wouldn't have to be blamed for anything. When I took the money to her she frowned at it as if I should have raised more. The way she looked at the money I raised was like she was disappointed. I looked away for a moment in order to keep my composure because I felt like screaming and crying based on the humiliation I experienced during the course of the last hour.

She didn't ask me how I was doing or how I felt but I told her anyway. I told her that I saw a few of my peers in some of the cars and they were laughing at me. Fighting back tears from the experience while also anticipating what hell I would have to endure tomorrow when I came into contact with those peers. None of this appeared to gain her attention as she looked at me and told me, "*I don't give a fuck, who are they?*" A part of me wanted to remind her who they were and how it was affecting me, but I swallowed it down and soothed myself by telling myself that better days are ahead. Seeing that my feelings didn't matter to her I moved on.

I did, however, ask her if she was going to go get their diapers and juice or if she wanted me to, and she replied, *"They have enough to last the night, just go across the street and get a pack of Jell-O and make them some Jell-O water."* It was as if there was a great disconnect, she didn't care about what I had gone through and probably never had any intention to use that money for good.

It took all I had not to scream and burst out crying because I had already told her that they had enough to last the night. How dare she send me to humiliate myself amongst my peers and their families to beg for money. But I wish that was the end of that night. After I got myself together, I came down stairs and asked for the money. She handed me about $7.00 and said, *"Get one box of Jell-O and buy me a pack of cigarettes."* I paused as I reached for the money, a frown on my face and my back tilted a little. I said *"Huh?"* She repeated herself as if what she said was right. I took the money and bought her cigarettes and the pack of Jell-O. The next day I woke up to her and the money missing. I used towels when the diapers ran out, and the Jell-O water was gone by the next afternoon. She returned late that night, but no diapers or juice in hand. Telling her that they needed diapers and more juice appeared to fall on deaf ears because she didn't respond at all.

✱✱✱

My earliest memory was around the age of three and what I mostly remember is loving every moment that I was with my mama. She gave me a sense of security, made me feel like everything was alright. I wanted to be with her all the time, and I do mean all the time. Whenever she left me to go hang out with her friends, or go anywhere, I would cry for her. I would cry so much that people would try and convince her to take me with her, because if she didn't I would ruin the night by crying and interfering with their nightly fun. I can recall always feeling a sense of want for her. It was almost as if I could sense when she was preparing to go out because all of a sudden my stomach would ache and

I'd feel the need to sit by her. I am not sure if this issue I had was due to the domestic violence between her and my father, as I don't know which came first. What I do know is that I felt a need to protect her. One of the clearest memories during this period was when I witnessed my father beating my mother one night, and seeing her go down and being hurt crushed me. I could never forget the way my father hit her and she fell into my playschool slide that was in the dining room area. I still can hear the sounds and how I felt that night! I remember screaming, *"You made mama break my slide."* When he hit her it went through my body! Out of that I knew I wanted to be near her because I did not want anybody hitting her again. I am uncertain if part of the reason I felt so close to my mother was due to the stories I heard her telling people about how she almost lost me several times when I was born. She used to say that I was her miracle child because I had died in her arms. I just felt a special connection to her.

When I went to preschool I am pretty sure the teachers were unhappy to see me on the days I attended. From the time I was able to see the school campus from the car, the tears would flow. I put on a full production every time they dropped me off. Sobbing, stiffening up, crying loudly, and begging her not to leave me was a regular occurrence. I can recall the end of the day well. The teachers would grab the toy phone and pretend to call some of my classmates' parents and tell them how well their child did for the day, and I would ask if they were going to call my mom and they would say, *"No, you cried again."* I couldn't be mad at them; they were right. I would promise them that tomorrow would be different, but after a few times of hearing that, they wouldn't even respond. Looking back now, I don't see how they did it. I was a handful.

Over the years it was difficult for me to process how the person I once cried for, wanted to protect, and loved beyond comprehension could treat me the way she did. She told me she loved me many times, but when events like the ones described so far took place, it caused me to start to fall into a place where I felt depressed, angry, and confused. Things within my household got a lot worse, and I began to fall further and further into a place where hope was threatened. I wanted to die so bad that I was angry some mornings when I woke up to another day. Other times I wanted her dead. The sound of her voice would make me cringe. I felt like I had weights lying on my chest every day. Mentally I was between homicide and suicide, and having a hard time figuring out which one would be worse. Sometimes standing in my upstairs window, I could imagine how quickly I would die if I jumped. I literally had to talk myself off the ledge. My fear of waking up in Hell often helped me to decide to live. Times when I was certain I would kill her, the thought of prison didn't sound so bad. However, my faith in God would somehow kick in and I would let the thought and plan go.

Notes

Piece 4

Hungry Again

Earlier today after arriving home from school I entered the apartment and I tested the waters by saying, *"Hi Mama."* She looks over at me, but she says nothing. I smile and head to my room. I am happy for a moment that she didn't have a list of things for me to do. That was wishful thinking, or maybe she is just trying to make me mad again because she waits until I get upstairs to my room and then I hear her call for me, *"Bitch get your ass down here and see what the fuck I want."* I was called bitch, whore, and tramp so regularly that I answered to them. I race downstairs and I stand in the doorway entrance between the hallway and the living room. There she is, cigarette in her hand, legs wide open, and of course, she is butt naked. She starts in with her problems, *"Bitch what the fuck are you doing upstairs when the food needs to be cooked?"* I swallow and take a deep breath before I respond. I say, *"Mama, what do you want me to cook?"* She looks at me with disgust and says, *"What the fuck do you think, the meat is in the sink."* I then ask softly, *"Do I get to eat this time?"* She's still looking at me with disgust on her face and says, *"Yeah."* Feeling okay, but still uneasy about when I get to eat (because there were many times I had to eat my food after everyone else was finished eating), I ask her if I get to eat when the food is hot and before the roaches get on it. I asked this question because in the past I have cooked dinner for her and my five younger siblings, only to eat after I've served everyone. Other times I couldn't eat until I cleaned the entire kitchen. This would be okay if there was a microwave, or if the apartment we lived in was not infested with roaches, but it was! I went to bed hungry many nights after cooking food for everyone because my plate would be covered with about 20 roaches by the time I finished washing the dishes, stove, and sweeping the kitchen and mopping. But tonight she told me that I could eat my food hot and boy was I excited.

Eating food hot became one of my main desires. So I cooked the food with the expectation that I would be able to eat the food I cooked while it was hot. I was excited as I cooked the food, and I felt accomplished in speaking up and negotiating getting to eat my dinner with everyone else. But, as I should have expected, this wouldn't happen.

So, I finished cooking dinner, served her, served them, and then I made my plate. It smelled good and I could see the heat rising from my plate. I made sure she had her ice and soda and I assured her that the kids have all their needs met. *Yes,* I am thinking to myself, *you finally get to eat*! Inside I am doing the happy dance and my mouth is salivating. They can't see it, but I am smiling from ear to ear on the inside. I can almost taste the chicken, macaroni, and that sweet cornbread. I had cut myself a corner piece and I cannot wait. I get ready to sit down and she calls me. Hoping that this will be quick I respond, *"Yes mama?"* She then says,*"Is the kitchen clean?"* I am thinking, of course not and you know it because I just finished cooking, but I dare not say that out loud. I respond by telling her that it is not cleaned yet, all while assuring her that it will be cleaned just how she likes it. I wonder why she is even asking. I clean the kitchen every night. She then directs me to get it cleaned. I remind her of our agreement and then she drops the bomb on me. She did it again! She tricked me! She promised this time that she would let me eat some of the food I cooked before the roaches crawl on it. I just finished making macaroni and cheese, fried chicken and cornbread, and I am still going to be hungry. She yells to me, *"Put it in the oven and the roaches won't get it."* I began to think and want to say out loud: I don't know about you, but last time I checked, the roaches get into everything from the television, oven, refrigerator, and many other places. I am floored, to say the least, because I have seen the roaches in there too, and once you turn on the oven, they come running out! So here we go. I try to negotiate eating my food now, all while looking at it and hoping I can at least taste it before the roaches do, but she is no longer responding to me. Tears well up in my eyes. I feel duped once again. I am hotter than a firecracker and every part of me wants to rebel and sit down and eat my food. But I don't. I put the plate in the oven and I cleaned the kitchen. Of course when I am done my food is no good because the oven roaches had a feast on it. Feeling completely defeated and angry at myself for falling for her tricks again, I put the kids to bed and I retreat to my room hungry once again.

That night I cried until it hurt almost as bad as the hunger pains. Although I had felt this pain many nights, I was not ready for the ones that were on their way tonight. I just couldn't understand it, why would she treat me like this? Why does she deny me the opportunity to eat, especially when I cooked it? I prayed and cried out asking why this is constantly happening to me? I tried to understand her rationale, but no matter what it just did not make sense. By the time I finished crying I was angry with both her and myself. When it was all over I decided that I wasn't going to cook for her or the kids again without at least sneaking a piece of something for myself. I struggled with this decision for a moment, because I was raised in the church, and you are supposed to honor and obey your parents. I struggled for a while, but eventually I had to forgive myself for taking a bite here and there, all while also praying that God would understand and cut me a break.

I continued to struggle with my faith in God and people. I struggled daily, wrestling with who I was by nature and who I felt I should be. I started to hate myself and I wanted to change. I worked very hard during this time to change who I was as a person because I felt like a punk and a baby. I felt like I was weak because I fell for the trap every time. I hated the fact that I was the way I was. I wanted to be mean and evil. I wanted to turn my emotions off. I tried to be different but I kept failing. I would wake up, tell myself that I wasn't going to help anybody, and that would last until I heard one of the kids asking for my help. Although I wanted to, I couldn't do it. I couldn't shut down and ignore them the way she ignored me. But I didn't give up trying because I felt like if I could just change who I was, she wouldn't treat me this way.

Notes

Piece 5

Flashlight

I t's dark with nothing but the streetlights and the moonlight competing for my attention as I try to fall asleep. I figure it's getting late because the noise from outside is becoming less and less. I take a moment to reflect on the day and drift in and out of my hopes for the future. I am thinking about all the things I will eat and places I will go when I am an adult. I also picture a life where I don't have to hide bruises or make up stories as to how I got them when I forgot to cover one. After my usual daydreaming I feel heaviness in my eyes and realize that it's finally happening, sleep is on its way. I drift away. Suddenly I hear voices and I open one eye and realize that it's still dark outside. I try to tune it out but the chatter was too close for me to drown it out. Then I start to think they may be here for me. So I try to recall the problems from earlier today. Nothing comes to mind, so I close my eyes and hope that it's not them again! The cops, I hope it's not them downstairs, because if it is, that means I am going to be called downstairs to watch her perform again. A few minutes pass by and I breathe a sigh of relief because by now she would have called me downstairs, but she hadn't. I drift back to sleep, only to be awakened by a different light this time. I hear male voices commanding me to get up. I take a second to try and wrap my mind around what is going on, because in the past they never came in my room. He is yelling for me to get up as if it's a sunny day and I was prepared for him. The light is getting closer and the voice is elevating, telling me to get up! The tone of voice is that of someone who is upset and has been inconvenienced. It's hard for me to see how many people are in my room because the lights continue to be flashed in my face. Finally I sit up on the sofa and look at them. Oh, now it makes sense! There she is in the background, crying and saying some of the same old lines: she's rebellious, she won't listen. The officer in charge begins to fuss at me, telling me how appreciative I should be to have a mom like her. Telling me how horrible my father is, and how I better do what she says. This officer is talking to me as if he knows me. He continues on as if he had all the information he needed. I am puzzled a bit because I had not seen my father for a while, and did not know how any of this made sense. Clearly it was the middle of the night, and there is nothing that a teenager should be doing in the middle of the night other than sleeping. But he continues to talk at me, all the while the flashlight is still pointed in my direction. Never once did he ask me what happened, and to tell you the truth at that time of night, I too did not know what happened that caused him to be in my room reminding me of the things I have to be thankful for.

He continued on for several minutes, at times threatening me. He stated several times that he would "bust a hole in the wall and arrest you for doing it." He went on to say that I don't want a piece of juvenile hall because girls in there would whoop my ass and even rape me. He continued on, all the while she is behind him and his partner. No longer did she have those fake tears running down her face nor the tremble in her voice. She was silently looking at me with a smirk on her face. She was happy and had no problem with him talking to me like that. Hell, this is the reason she called him. Nevertheless, he told me that he was going to make me a promise that if he had to come out to my home again he would bust a hole in the wall and arrest me. He went on to say that I better hope he never comes back or I was leaving with him. His name was Officer Cox. Prior to him leaving, he never once asked me about me, all he did was ask questions and answer them for himself, like who fed me and who took care of me. Little did he know I ate at school, fed siblings, attended parent teacher conferences, paid the rent, grocery shopped and many other adult tasks, so in essence, financially the County took care of me, and I handled the rest.

Over the course of about a year I had encounters with many officers, sometimes multiple times in the same day. My mother would call the police or have one of my siblings call whenever I disobeyed her or "rebelled." For the life of me I never understood why they never took her to jail for misusing 911 or calling the station with the same issue. Initially I respected law enforcement and understood their responsibility to come when they were called, but after getting to know some of them by name and them knowing the story she was about to tell, I lost hope in them. Many of them berated me and made me feel smaller than an ant, hardly ever questioning me alone or asking the right questions. I have to give it to them though, with the performance she put on, who wouldn't believe that this lady wasn't doing the best she could to single-handedly raise her children after their fathers abandoned them. It was tough, but after experiencing this for about six months, the screaming, lights flashing in my eyes, threats, and yelling became normal and I became numb to it. It was almost like I was invisible to the police because they looked right through me and delivered me a speech or harsh warning about the consequences for

my actions.

Notes

TOPIC: _____

Piece 6

One Piece

I t's a hot sunny day and my mother along with me and my five siblings are out running her errands. We have been in this car for hours and would like to get out. She pulls up to the fish market, parks in the red, and tells me to get out and go get the owner. The smell of the deep fried fish hits me like a ton of bricks and my mouth and belly want some. I get the nice man and he comes out to the car to talk to her. I get back in the car and she talks to him for about a good five minutes before giving him her order and asking for him to fill it on "credit." He pauses, with the ticket order paper already completely filled out. He tells her no and reminds her of the last time he gave her fish on "credit" and how he cannot do this for her again. Then she starts to wear him down. She starts in with how hard life is for her, and how she will pay him interest when she gets her food stamps. He asks her how much she needs and she turns and points at all of us, laying it on thick how we had not eaten all day and she needed to feed her kids. He looks into the car at us while they continue to negotiate the terms of the deal. They go back and forth for another five minutes or so before he caves and agrees to give her a few pounds of red snapper.

We sit there and the level of excitement increases for me. And here they come, the golden fish in the red and white paper trays covered with that glistening white paper-type stuff. The oil is glistening on that paper and we are ready to chow down. She thanks him over and over again, and I thank him too. She reaches into the tray and grabs a napkin and hands me one piece and says, *"Pass this back."* I pass it all the way back in the station wagon and I look back for the next piece, and the next piece. I'm turning around to get the rest, because thus far she has only passed back three pieces and there are three of us left to get a piece. Then I see her put the tray in front of her and let out a sigh while saying, *"Woo I am hungry."* Puzzled I wait a second before inquiring about the other three pieces.

Then I watch in slow motion as she takes a bite, I promise you I saw the heat rise after she bit into it. I then ask her for the rest of the pieces as if she cannot count. She then turns around, looks at me and says, *"I gave three pieces. You guys split them."* She turns around as if what she said was right, and continues on eating several pieces. I quickly turn around and grab the fish that was left and split it between us all. Of course by then those of us who did not originally receive a piece were only able to get a bite.

I was pissed and disgusted all at the same time. I was hot as hell, how could she do that right in front of our faces?! It was as if she thought I was stupid, like I couldn't recall her conversation with this man prior to him agreeing to give us the fish.

He agreed because he wanted us (the kids) to eat. Several of my siblings in the car asked for more, but it was as though she was deaf because she continued devouring that fish. After watching her eat piece after piece I turned my head and promised myself I would never do that to my kids.

Notes

Piece 7

Hard

Life was hard. Being hungry was painful but being isolated was worse. Not being allowed access to food had its sting, but after being hungry so often, I learned to put it out of my mind. I would tell myself that I was not hungry while hearing the rumbling of my stomach. I would sometimes sit in the window and smell the food from outside and swallow, pretending that I had eaten the food. Overcoming isolation was a much more difficult task to conquer.

Sitting in my room day in and day out, being ignored or having negative statements hurled at me did a number on me when I was alone. It was almost like a song being played over and over again. You know the words and the tune but you cannot turn it off. When I would sit in my room I would hear something like this: you ain't nothing, you're a dumb mutha-fucka, stupid ass, whore, you ain't shit bitch, bitch who do you think you are, your dumb ass...words like this and many others would run through my mind. I would find myself crying until it hurt, falling asleep crying and hearing myself crying and moaning in my sleep. The pain ran so deep that at times I thought I was going to die from the internal pain of having my heart ripped out and stomped on by the person I loved the most.

I would close my eyes at times and pretend that I was blind to what was really going on. In my mind I would envision the life that I wanted and felt I deserved. Within this darkness I found light. Being blind was the same as me being isolated, restricted from something. That in which I had no control over. I started taking into account what I did have access to and making a big deal about these things. I strengthened my sense of smell as I would sit in the window, eyes closed and identify where the food was being cooked and what type of food it was. I would use my ears to tell me what was going on outside, and I would create the narrative. For instance, I would hear a lady talking and I would make up that she is talking nicely to her child, telling her that she could be anything she wanted to be in life. I would hear a man and I would imagine that he was happily talking with his wife and treating her with dignity and respect. This may sound crazy, but it is how I began to survive. I would switch off at times and pretend I was deaf. This would work great when I would be called downstairs to be humiliated and hit. I would turn my ears off and imagine that she was saying the things I wanted to hear. Being deaf was much harder than being blind, because it is hard to tap out on hearing because you really cannot shut your ears the way you can shut your eyes. Nevertheless, I did the best I could. I looked at my mother with ease as if the words she was saying were not hurting me. In my room when I was pretending to be deaf this allowed me to turn off the negative songs in my head. I would then use my pen/pencil to write down positive things about myself. As I was writing them I could hear them in my head, and at times I would notice that as long as I was writing, I could hear what I wanted, and it allowed the other songs to stop playing for a little while. Also, my elective in school was typing at the time, and we were given a typing sheet that had the layout of the keyboard. I would sit in my room and practice typing on this sheet of paper, "Tracy is the best". I incorporated this during my times of isolation or to combat the negative songs being played in my head. I had to make several of those sheets out of blank paper because I would type on it so much that it would rip. I was also enrolled in a Friday class of crocheting and knitting. Because I didn't attend regularly I did not know how to complete the patterns correctly. But that did not stop me. I would sit in that room and go to town with the needle. I sometimes drowned the negativity out by consuming my time with typing on a sheet of paper, repeating positive words, reciting scriptures, and crocheting.

The beatings from my mother increased from maybe once a week to almost daily, and at times multiple times a day. I wasn't sure if this was due to my new response to her antics because I did not cry or flinch as much when she hit me because I was tapped out, and I think this pissed her off. I went full days without eating and only having access to my room and the bathroom. Sometimes I would suck on a piece of paper in order to rid my mouth of the dry taste it had developed. I wasn't allowed to go downstairs without being summoned or when I was cooking or cleaning. To hurt my feelings and get a reaction, she would encourage my siblings to ignore me, and the little ones who relied on me for everything she punished them by making them sit next to her when I was allowed out of my room.

I could hear them cry from my room and this was difficult for me to tune out. However, what hurt me the most was when I heard her hitting them for crying for me. It hurt me to my core because they were babies who were used to relying on me for their bottles, diaper changes, food, and comfort. I used to rock them to sleep and take care of them like a parent. So denying them access to me made me angry and hurt my feelings. I really had to turn to God and reading my bible in order to deal with some of the discomfort her actions caused. I would lay and cry and rely heavily on scriptures that said "all things are working for me" and "it was good that I was afflicted." Knowing that God would never leave me nor forsake me gave me comfort to push through these times. I held on strongly to my faith that these times in my life would be beneficial one day. I was strong and no one could tell me otherwise.

This was a lot for a 12 or 13 year old. No child this age is supposed to be worried about things like what outfit they are going to wear to school the next day, what snack they want to eat, or something else that kids make a huge deal over. But for me, I had to spend time navigating through what felt like hell on earth.

I believe that my mother isolated me at times because I challenged her. I would ask her questions and I stopped agreeing with her. Prior to reaching this place in my teens, I would keep my mouth shut when I witnessed her manipulating people out of their money. I got tired of pretending I was blind, and I started asking questions. My mom did not like being questioned, especially when it was about her actions. I asked her why she would have me tell her friends she wasn't home when she knew they were there to get their money back. She also didn't like when we returned home from church and I reminded her about what the preacher and the bible said. At times I told her that the way she was hurting me was not godly!

The consequences were isolation. I was belittled for betraying her and not being on her side if we did not agree about something.

Notes

Piece 8

The Training

F rom a very young age I had been told several times: if someone hits you, you better hit them back. If they hurt you and you need help, look for the nearest brick or bottle and bust them over the head with it.

So there I was, dressed with my hair done and about to start school. I entered the gate that separated me from my siblings and I walked into my class. I kept telling myself that everything is going to be okay and that I am going to have fun at this place. I checked out the scene and there was a big carpet that was colorful, pictures of the alphabet on the walls. Yes, I am in kindergarten. I managed to sit down like all the rest of the kids, but honestly the lessons were boring. They were introducing kids to letters that I had mastered the weekend before. I observed how patient the teacher was when she engaged with the students, and I reflected on how my experience was learning the alphabet. It was nothing like this, there was no belt, no crying, and no yelling, yet at the same time I learned it much faster than these kids. I think the first few days were okay, as I played outside during recess and enjoyed my time with Tyrone. Tyrone was tall and could reach stuff that a shorty like me couldn't.

He was friendly and enjoyed playing with the big red ball that was hard to grab but fun to bounce. It seemed like recess lasted forever because I remember laughing and running around with Tyrone. Things were going well until Jose came up and took the ball from Tyrone. Tyrone made the usual comments, "give it back, I had it first." But Jose wouldn't give the ball back. In the meantime, I was standing there becoming heated and wanting to get involved and make Jose give us the ball back, but I remembered what mama said about only answering if I was called. That meant that I was not supposed to go looking for trouble or involve myself in someone else's mess unless they called or needed me. I understood that unless someone was hurting me or someone I cared about, I needed to stay out of it. For the first few minutes I stuck to the rules, but I felt compelled to intervene when I could see that Tyrone was becoming upset. Jose had started calling names and apparently hurting Tyrone's feelings which was then hurting mine.

A moment or two later Jose hits Tyrone! That's it, that's all I need to jump in, and I do! I run up on Jose, telling him that *we had the ball first* and that he better give Tyrone back the ball. Jose, looking at me and clearly sizing me up, then decides to punch me in the stomach! What did he do that for! I thought. He is going to regret this! I'm hunched over from the impact of the blow to my stomach and tears are welling up in my eyes. I am stuck for a moment as my blurry eyes are scanning the playground looking for the nearest brick or bottle to bust Jose over the head with. To my surprise there aren't any bricks or bottles within the gates of the kindergarten area. Still bent over I am thinking and crying, thinking and crying. Then when I find the strength I launch at Jose and I sink my teeth into his shoulder, holding on for dear life just like a pitbull.

For a few seconds all I can hear is Jose screaming, I cannot see much because my eyes are still full of tears. A few more seconds and the teachers were screaming for me to let go, let go. They screamed this over and over again until I realized that one of them had me lifted off the ground and was trying to pull me off of Jose's shoulder. But none of their efforts worked. I was still biting Jose for what he did to Tyrone and me. I heard him screaming from the pain but that wasn't satisfying enough for me, I wanted him to hurt the way he hurt me and Tyrone, so I held on for a little while longer. When it was all said and done, I heard Jose crying and the teachers screaming for assistance because Jose was bleeding from me digging my teeth into his shoulder. Jose had to be taken to the hospital or doctor's office to be checked out.

Unfortunately for me, my cuteness and charisma would not be good enough to keep these teachers from hating me. After walking me to the classroom I saw the way they looked at me like I was an animal or something. One of them came over to me to tell me how bad biting someone was, and how I was in big trouble in school and at home.

Every time I tried to tell them my side they just shut me down, reminding me how Jose was bleeding and how bad my behavior was. I cried but they didn't care, all they wanted to do was point out how I had hurt Jose. No one thought about Tyrone or me, hell, where were they when Jose came up and started bullying us? Did they not see Tyrone crying, or me bent over after being punched in the stomach? What was so good about Jose, his screaming? Was that where I went wrong, should I have screamed?

I heard the teachers talking among each other as if I wasn't in the room. I would have had to be deaf not to hear them talk about how tight my grip was on that poor kid's shoulder and how they didn't want to put up with stuff like this all year. During lunchtime they isolated me as if I attacked Jose for no reason and the other kids were in danger. Huh, all I knew was that I needed to talk to my mama about what else she would suggest I bust someone over the head with if there isn't a brick or bottle available. I ate my lunch, cried some more, took a nap, and attempted several times to tell them how it all started, but noooooo, they didn't want to hear it. A few times they tried to make me feel bad for him, coming over and asking me if I was sorry for hurting Jose. I would politely tell them no and try to tell them why, but based on me not being sorry, they dismissed me and wouldn't hear a word.

That was my last day of kindergarten because when my mother arrived, they tried to prevent me from running to her car because they needed to talk to her about my suspension. Little did they know, you don't keep my mother's kids from her unless you are ready to be bitten with her words and maybe her hands. They learned the hard way because they wouldn't let me out of the office. When my mother screamed from her car that I better get my ass in her car, I dismissed myself because I was not about to catch her wrath. After I told my mother what happened, she told me that I did the right thing, but encouraged me to use my fist the next time because people are dirty and I could have caught something.

The meeting with the school was very eventful for me. The teachers and the principal showed up with their evidence of my attack on Jose and the issues they had with her lack of cooperation when she came to pick me up. What they didn't expect was for my mother to have her own plan of action. She jumped right in, scolding them about where they failed to protect her child and the other kid involved (Tyrone). She laid it out! She pointed out how they failed to hear me out, and she made it clear that I never attack anyone for no reason. She told them that if I bit the boy it was because he did something to me first. You can only imagine the looks on their faces because they were not ready for her. She told them the boy was lucky that I didn't get my hands on a brick or bottle. These people could not believe what she saying. She also admonished them about how they isolated me all day and how wrong they were for that. By the end of the meeting it was clear that kindergarten was not a good fit for me. My mother and I had already talked about what kindergarten was supposed to teach me and how I was already far ahead of the kids. The teachers and the principal had no argument with her. I think they knew it was in their students' and their own best interests.

That day I was proud of my mom. I was proud that she defended me. Although it was not the most conventional way of handling things, in my home this was great. It served the same purpose but she used a different approach. Of course it would not have been okay for me to hit someone over the head with a brick or bottle, but the gist behind what she was saying was for me to defend myself, and whenever my own strength was not enough, to look for other avenues to protect myself. I can appreciate these teachings because they caused me to always assess my surroundings and to think fast.

Unfortunately, the way the teachers isolated me and silenced my voice was not cool at all. While my actions may have been seen as extreme, I should have been asked what happened to me. This event made me feel small and devalued, just as when the officers arrived at my home to scold me about my behavior without taking the time to assess the situation and ask me what happened. These events led me to believe that I didn't count, and my reasons behind my behavior didn't matter. It seemed like people could do whatever they wanted to do to me, but when I reacted and people got hurt, I was the bad one. From a very young age, instances like the ones I've described impacted me internally and sometimes made me feel like I should just shut up and take whatever was handed to me. Eventually I would shut up, however, once my button was pushed one too many times, I would explode. Sometimes that meant fights or destroying property. It would take years for me to make this connection and begin the process of speaking my truth even when no one wanted to hear it.

Around the age of 16, I knew that I had to change this behavior if I was going to succeed in life, so I utilized some of the skills learned in therapy to do so. Therapy along with spending a lot of time self-analyzing was extremely helpful. I would look back on times when I exploded and examine what was happening prior to this moment. I started paying attention to how I felt internally when people said or did things that I did not like. I started paying more attention to why those things bothered me. I learned to breathe and focus on me and what I was feeling, and then express myself to others. This was not an overnight success; it was the beginning of me learning to stay true to me, while also remaining in control of my actions.

Notes

TOPIC: _____

Piece 9

Random Acts of Kindness

Sometimes out of the blue my mother would call my name and ask me if I either wanted to go skating or swimming. For the most part I would say yes and happily spend a day alone. She would tell me to eat a sandwich or something and then drop me off at the pool or the skating rink. I would enter the pool area or skating rink all by myself and enjoy the few hours of peace. For the majority of the time I would find myself spending the first half hour simply unwinding, and by that I mean allowing myself to exhale my previous issues and breathe in the moment I was currently in. Following this I would either put the skates on or put my stuff in the pool locker room and jet out into paradise. I loved the act of skating and swimming, but most of all I loved the freedom I felt while I was doing it. I didn't have to look over my shoulder. I didn't have to wonder if I was about to be punched or kicked. I didn't have to wonder if I was going to have to take care of everybody. I could just simply enjoy some of the things that people my age enjoyed. I would stay to myself the majority of my time out, however, if I saw a group of kids who appeared friendly, I'd start a conversation with them and possibly join in on their fun.

At times I felt a bit out of place when some of the groups would ask me where my friends are, or their facial expressions and comments after I would tell them I was there alone getting a break from home. Poor regular kids. They had no idea what I was talking about and why anyone would be as happy as I was to be in a skating rink or swimming pool alone. Sometimes explaining a little bit about my dynamics would damper the mood for the kids, so I learned to stop going into detail and simply just tell them I was there because my mom let me.

Days like these for the most part ended without a problem. However, after some time of reflection in my room during isolation I would question the reasons why she took me to those places in the first place. I began to run the tapes back in my head, recalling what happened before she made me the offers to swim or skate, and also what words she used when asking and after.

Following my review I noticed that there was a pattern happening here. What I noticed was that the "random acts of kindness were not so random. The timing may have been out of nowhere, but the reasons behind them could be seen from a distance if I'd only paid attention. I began to realize that these offers would arrive during times when I was not crying much about anything, or when I appeared to be nonchalant about my daily struggles and would shut down from her emotionally.

My mother could read a person like none other, and when I say read them, I mean she had an idea about what they were about, their motives, weaknesses, and desires. She was able to figure people out rather quickly. When my mother was unable to figure someone out, she was uneasy. Based on my observations, when I would withdraw myself from her emotionally and simply just be going through the motions, she could not handle it. It was during these times where she would call me down and tell me she wanted to "give me a break" or "let me have some fun." The light in my eyes when she would offer up the skating rink or swimming was her way to get me to let her back in.

So basically this was never really for me because, let's face it, I would not have needed a break if she was taking care of her own children, cooking for her household, attending her kids' parent teacher conferences, and doing all the other parent duties that she forced me to do every day.

Unfortunately once I realized this, I no longer accepted her offers. How could I? How could I accept something in order for her to feel better? I couldn't accept anymore because I was not letting her off the hook, and I realized that although those moments were fun, they were tools being used to get me back to a place I had been working hard to stay away from.

Notes

Piece 10

He's Back

It's a nice sunny day outside and I am determined to enjoy it. Ever since the two good officers Tolbert and Walker came by, and as long as I clean the house and make sure the little ones are good, I am free! Since I got up early this morning to get it all done, she will have no excuse to hold me in here today.

I am rumbling through bags of lightly dirtied clothes. I go through the smell test and finally I find the red jumpsuit thing that doesn't smell too bad. I put it on and head downstairs. I have it all figured out, I am going to hit the corner quick as I come down, and I am going right out the back door, or so I thought.

As soon as I hit the last stair I hear her. *"Where the fuck do you think you are going?"* Determined to have a good day I respond, *"Outside Mama."* *"No the fuck you not, you gone get my mutha-fuckin house cleaned."* I answered her as politely and softly as I could, *"I did Mama, I got up early and did it."* She runs through everything I am supposed to do: the bathrooms, sweeping the stairs, cleaning the kitchen, changing the kids' diapers, mopping the kitchen and dining room…I said yes to them all because I had done them.

Although there is silence, I sense that this conversation isn't over. She then starts in on me about how I wasn't leaving anywhere until she said so. I remind her of the deal she made with Officers Walker and Tolbert. She jumps up from the couch, and for some reason I didn't run. She is in my face and I am on the last stair before reaching downstairs. I am looking down, hoping that she does not have on all of her rings. Unfortunately she does; just about every finger has a ring on it, and the nugget ring is one of them. I am frozen, I can't look up, I can't say anything, and I am just waiting to see what move she chooses today. From where she is standing she could knee me, punch me, grab me by my hair, or punch me dead in the face. She has me wide open. She begins to tell me again that I am not going a mutha-fuckin place unless she says so. My eyes fill up with tears because this is not part of the deal. And although she has broken deals before, today I am determined to go outside and enjoy my day. I have had enough and figure that beat-up or not, I wanted to go outside.

I open my mouth and remind her again of the deal. Slap, slap, push, and there I am, laid on my back on the stairs with her knee in my stomach. I can't breathe! A part of me is fading, but another part is screaming for me to protect myself. I open my eyes to reconnect to what is happening to me, and I realize that she has messed my hair up, is punching me in the head, and her knee is only letting up for short moments because I am struggling with her. My body was moving from side to side. I am not sure if it's because her knee is in my stomach and is preventing me from staying engaged, but for a moment I am just dazed.

I hear a voice screaming, calling out to God, and pleading for her to stop. It took me a second to realize it, but the voice I hear is mine. She loses her balance and clearly is exhausted from her minute of punching and snatching my hair. She stands up and my voice is still going. Now I hear it saying, *"Satan the Lord rebuke you."* I heard the pastor tell the church to say this when they feel the devil is using their loved ones to hurt them. Clearly she had an issue with this, because I see her face and she is looking me dead in my eyes with disbelief. She then starts calling me bitch and says she has something else for me. I see her fixing her rings and I knew within my heart she was coming for my face. There was no way I was going to let this happen again, last time she scraped the stitches out of my cheek with her ring.

I react quickly as she lunges for me, and my knees block her. She bounces back after running into my bent legs. The momentum or her being out of shape must have dazed her a bit. I am not sure if my feet getting up that high made an impact on her body or her mind, but either way you would have thought she won the lottery. She began to scream, *"Go call the police, she did it this time, she finally hit me."* Confused, I tell her that she is the one who hit me, and that I simply blocked her because I was not taking a hit from her fist full of rings again.

It is as if I said nothing, because she continues to encourage a member of the household to go call the police. She seemed happy. I did what I could to fix my hair and leave. I went to my best friend's apartment two doors away. As soon as she and her family saw me, they brought me in and hugged me. I was an emotional wreck. Scared that the police will only believe her. Scared that the knots that were probably forming on my head wouldn't be looked at. I was wondering if I should have just let her hit me with her fist full of rings. At least then I would have proof of the struggle.

Almost an hour goes by, and nothing. My friends were confident that the police would not do anything to me. But they didn't know the threat Officer Cox had made that night, and they didn't know that the other members of the house would lie for her if they had to. I was scared; as all I could think of is how bad juvenile hall was going to be, and the hell the babies would go through if they didn't have me there to take care of them.

The familiar sound of an officer's radio sounded like it was being played on a loudspeaker because it went through my heart. I can never forget that moment. There he was, Officer Cox. He was at my friend's door reminding me what he had promised all those nights ago. He made me walk to him, he told me to turn around and put my hands behind my back and then it happened: the cuffs locked.

In that moment, all I could think of was what the babies would do without me. Who would feed them, panhandle for them, cook for them, and shield

them from whoopings? Who would wrap them up

like a burrito at night so that the roaches wouldn't

get in their ears? Who would wake the rest of them

up, get them ready for school, and attend their

school meetings. How would they eat when she

disappeared? In that moment I hated her for taking

me away from them, especially knowing that they

depended on me.

Officer placed me in the back of that car as if

it was his pleasure. As we were passing my mother,

I remember her crying and saying that her heart was

hurting. At that moment I was certain she had no

heart. I also thought about the times I wanted to

harm her. I thought about earlier that day, asking

myself if I should have earned being in the back of

this police cruiser. I struggled and I struggled hard

to remind myself that I had done the right thing by

not hitting or harming my mother. Officer Cox had

a look of satisfaction on his face, and again, he

never asked me anything.

Notes

Piece 11

Damaged Goods

When I was very little I can remember being called the "ABC baby" by some of my mom's friends. I can remember performing for her friends and my family. I was very active in elementary school, as I was part of the drill team and got the chance to participate in the community parade. If someone put a record on or turned on Soul Train, that was all she wrote! I could not contain myself. I loved to dance and sing. I was bubbly and always full of energy. I sang in my second grade class talent show, danced in a school talent show, and loved being involved in everything! I have to say that the energetic, motivated, and confident person I am today existed from the beginning. And although events in my life would challenge me at my core, I am grateful that I survived. I know that being aware of who I was from the beginning helped me endure the events that took place a little later in my life. When my life was challenging, I did everything I could to hold on to this part of me.

I can remember the struggles in school academically, always being behind my peers because I didn't attend school regularly, or I was catching up on sleep during class. I can remember feeling like a fish out of water. The tears in my eyes then birthed what I needed to continue. I can remember being teased for wearing dirty clothes and wearing the same outfit twice. It was during those days that I thought about my future children and vowed that they would not have these experiences. I can remember being left on the playground with no one to play with, and it was in those times that I purposed to have children who would love others. During those times I also vowed not to treat people that way. I can remember how hard it was to go to school after my peers witnessed me panhandling, and I knew my future was going to be better than that. I can remember watching my mother manipulate people out of their rent money and other things, and it was then that I vowed to use my powers for good. These events had the ability to break me but I was not built that way.

These experiences taught me to learn from every situation. Compassion for others was already a part of who I was, but it was refined within these moments. Although I was hurting, I knew it was not always going to be this way. I decided that there was a way for me to find value in every situation. Whether it was learning what to do, or what not to do, I was dedicated to learning and making it worth my while. I also learned that there are some things that isolation produced that integration didn't. It creates a space where one can be centered. While in isolation I could gather my thoughts and analyze what was happening in my life because there wasn't much interference from outside sources. It is there where I developed the ability to separate myself from my circumstances. Being able to do this released some of the stress when I was on the verge of losing my mind.

Now reflecting on this so many years later, it flows so easily. However, at the time when this was taking place, I could not articulate what I was doing. At that time I was simply trying to keep myself from going crazy and I was trying to keep my composure. I reflect now and I can see what my strategies were at that time and how I survived. I am so grateful to God because at the age of 12 and 13 there was no way I could have done that by myself. I am a fighter in every sense of the word and I don't think I would be who I am today absent of these experiences.

Over the years I have had the amazing opportunity of working with people at their worst and being able to demonstrate love and compassion that have contributed to their lives. I cannot forget where I came from and how I felt all those years ago. I am grateful for those moments of sadness and despair. I know what it feels like to be hopeless and/or invisible. I recognize this feeling when I meet people at work or in my community and I connect with that part of them without making them feel less than. I aim to give people what I needed when I was in that place.

Notes

TOPIC: _____

Piece 12

Relationships

E very day I strive to grow in areas of need. Identifying these areas can sometimes be difficult. Studies show that children who experience abuse and neglect are at a higher risk of having issues emotionally, behaviorally, and socially. I can attest to this as it relates to my ability to maintain relationships. I believe that the trauma I experienced hindered my ability to manage relationships properly.

My identity and self-worth laid in the hands of my mother. Until around the age of 13, I was stuck there. I did not know how to maintain my newfound independence and felt the need to still be validated by someone. So, over the years I passed the validation power from one person to another. There was always someone I admired, and I would give this authority to them. At times it was a foster mother, group home workers, supervisors, mentors, and the list goes on. I wanted to please them in hopes that they would love me and see me the way I longed for my mother to. This would go on for years and not only with the identified person. I would choose friends I felt had a void that I could fill while having qualities to fill my void as well. To say the least, this was a recipe for disaster.

Disappointment after disappointment was a road I seemed to live on. I struggled hard for years, because I didn't know how to fix the relationship or end it properly. This was directly related to my relationship with my mother. She would reject me by ignoring me or telling me I wasn't her daughter.

So I found myself looking for validation and someone to say they could see me. I was looking for them to not only see me, but to see me beyond what I told them. I wanted them to see how much trust I was placing in them. I tried showing them how much I needed a hero the way I was everyone else's hero. Eventually I realized I was signing them up without their consent. You see, they had no idea what holes or shoes they were being cast to fill. As a result of my arrested development emotionally and socially, I found myself in unhealthy relationships and I didn't know how to terminate them. So I resorted to what I knew, rejection.

Rejection showed up a bit differently in the relationships I developed, yet the same. When I perceived someone was treating me badly, hurt my feelings, ignored me, used me, or exploited me, I would try to prevent them from being rejected by me (cut off).

To help prevent this I would up my game by doing everything in my power to show them that they didn't want to lose me. I could be exhausted and I would instantly go to their aid. There were no limits to what I would do for them. They had access to me any day or time. I would inconvenience my marriage to be there for them. I would do this because I didn't want to lose them and I also knew the consequences of them hurting me. Once my anger peaked, it wasn't pleasant; it was quite vicious. However, at the moment of me disconnecting from the relationships, I felt justified. I felt like what they did to me justified my response. I was wrong. I say my behavior was different but it was the same as my mother's, because in the end I rejected people just as she rejected me.

I did not know how to disconnect without completely detaching. This was the only way I knew how to respond. Looking back I can see how this is what my mother did to me, and it hurt. Yet at the time my thought process was that they deserved to be cut off and disconnected from me. I had learned this when I finally cut my mother off at around the age of 15, and I felt she earned it. Needless to say, I needed to learn how to terminate relationships with dignity. I had to listen to my first mind and learn to accept people for who they were and do this without the thought that an encounter with me would change them.

Over the years, my perception of why people behaved the way they did towards me caused me to behave in a manner that I now know was inappropriate. I do not regret terminating past relationships; however, my approach could have been better. I don't regret them because many of them were toxic in more ways than one, and this was partially due to my mindset when these relationships began. I started many of them with unhealthy and unreasonable expectations. My behavior in these relationships set them up for failure from the beginning. I robbed people of the opportunity to choose me the way I chose them. I made them responsible for things that they could not truly fulfill, nor had an option to. I hid my desires and only presented them with the parts of me I could afford to let them see. I was dishonest and too afraid to show them the side of me that was vulnerable and starving for connection. Instead, what I presented was the strong one; the giver, the caregiver, and the one who appeared to have it together, so ultimately I created the lack of balance in the relationship. I also believe that at some point some of them were aware of this and took advantage of me. When I ended the relationships, I was coming from a place of hurt. A place where I felt violated on many levels.

To a certain degree I feel like I always knew this but could not connect the dots.

I finally made the connection following me terminating a sisterly relationship. I am not sure if it was the fact that this relationship had lasted more than 15 years and I had the data to dissect, but I know it was clear. I knew that I had been operating from a place where I would always be disappointed. I was setting my expectations of others based on who I was. I was also expecting them to value me in a way that I had yet to value myself! When this became clear to me, I had to seek help both spiritually and mentally. I needed to correct this before I could trust myself in another relationship. Not overnight, but over a season or two I was able to address these areas.

I had to see myself. All that time I was expecting others to see me when I was not seeing myself. I had to be who I had been for others for so long. I had to be my own caregiver and my own friend. I had to be my own hero and acknowledge that when I was isolated and hurting. I had been that to myself then. Realizing that I was what I needed all my life allowed me to take my power and be secure in knowing that when the chips are down, I can always count on me. After all, I had been doing this the whole time, but I was not giving myself credit for it.

Retiring

I cannot remember a year of school where I did not fight someone. I feel sorry for the people who baited me because little did they know that the beatdown I was getting ready to give them had more to do with me than them. I would set out to avoid problems just like my mother taught me, but my big mouth, over-the-top personality would almost always offend someone. My short stature was a false positive for my opponents because they thought that my height meant that they could win. I have to admit that when I was hurting my worst I would welcome the fights. I think it is even safe to say that once I knew a person didn't like me, I would bait them a bit by turning myself up a notch or two. If they didn't like my loud laughter, I would purposely watch a show that would tickle me deeply. I would let my voice rip through the house or room and get them going.

I matured in this area slightly during my teens due to a combination of things. I became more concerned about the people around me, as some of the teenagers in my group home were hurting emotionally and needed someone to support them, and I found helping them refreshing. It was quite difficult to fight the people I was mentoring. But I must admit that this was short lived, as this behavior resurfaced and continued until I was a mother. I was so ruthless that my husband, who was my boyfriend when we conceived our son, told me that he needed to ask me a question the night we found out we were going to be parents. This took me by surprise because my son was planned and we had already talked about waiting until after we lived together to discuss marriage further.

So here we are sitting in Red Lobster in Beverly Hills. I had to use the restroom prior to arriving, but I had to hold it until we were seated. I could see that he was in deep thought because he kept looking around and acting weird. Finally, he said, *"I need to ask you something,"* and tried to grab my hand. I immediately jumped up and told him I had to use the restroom. While in the restroom I wrestled with how I was going to tell him no if he asked me to marry him. Being that we were at a fancy dinner and all, I didn't want to spoil the mood and I wanted to remain excited about the baby, so I had to delay my time in the restroom until I could compose myself.

I exited the restroom, and as I am approaching the table I see my man with this nervous smile on his face and I couldn't help but think that I was about to break his little heart! Or so I thought. I sit down and he grabs my hand. He looks at me deep into my eyes and he says, *"I just have one request."* I look at him and I tell him, *"Okay."* He looks at me deeper and says, *"You know you're going to be a mom now, please stop fighting."* Of course I was pissed and snatched my hand back. I couldn't believe that this man was asking me such a thing. But then he reminded me of my last two fights, one that had just taken place a few weeks ago which meant I had already had a fight while I was pregnant. I promised him that I wouldn't fight again.

I wish I could say that I was able to keep that promise, but unfortunately I fought again when I was seven months pregnant. Not only did I fight, but the person I fought was a relative. To add insult to injury it was at a KFC on Mother's Day. This fight was similar to all the rest; I was arguing because I felt degraded and unaccepted by her. Rejection and my abandonment issues were all present that day. I couldn't keep my mouth closed to save my life during this period of my life. What I remember the most about that day was the statement she made about my mother not wanting me. Words like this cut like a knife. They cut deep not only because they were ugly words, but mainly because I believed them. When people would say things like this to me, my anger and outburst was only partially due to them attacking me, but the majority of it was because deep down I felt that they were right.

Purpose

The trauma that I experienced throughout my childhood turned out to be a setup for my future. Although I went through many painful days and nights, it continues to be worth it. I knew deep down inside of me that the hell I was experiencing had a purpose. What I did not know then was how it would shape my life and positively impact the lives of those I came into contact with. Little did I know that my experiences with law enforcement, judges, teachers, foster parents, and child welfare workers would be part of the foundation I speak to others from. The hopelessness I felt allows me to enter a room and feel it. I did not know that my being ignored or overlooked by many would open my eyes in ways that others cannot see. That I would be able to connect with individuals on a level that would cause the most educated to scratch their heads. I did not know how powerful my story would be, not because I had a story to tell, but because of the way I tell it. I never imagined that the very people who had ruled over my life at one point would be reading my reports. One of the best things is that because of what I went through as a child, I am able to look at all the mothers on my caseload and offer them a level of compassion that my mother never received. Grateful. Thankful. I am grateful for every storm, every burden I carried. I am grateful for every teacher that overlooked me and every person that looked at me and felt sorry for me. Because without that, I would not know how to operate effectively. I think that as a child I could not articulate what I am speaking now, however, I knew then that those things would be instrumental in my future.

Knowing what I know afforded me the opportunity to really meet people where they were. It also affords me the courage and ability to challenge them to grow. My life experiences prepared me for the life I was designed to live. My outlook on life has a unique lens in which I view the world. My lens has scratches, bends, and sees near and far. I can see in the dark, breathe underwater, fit into a box, float and swim, all without the usual equipment. I see possibility when others see no hope. I see tomorrow while others are figuring out today. When I work with children, I hear beyond what their mouths say. In addition to their body language, I hear their pain. I can see what they want to say, but cannot find the words. I also see the deep desires of those who work with marginal populations within child welfare and education. Their desire to help and the frustrations they begin to carry with them while interacting and serving their clients. The way that defeat drags behind them after they have given their best touches me. I see the pain and the impact that dealing with people who are hurting brings.

Notes

TOPIC: _____

Conclusion

Over the years I have been asked: Why didn't you run away, tell someone, eat before you fed everyone else, and what made you stay?

The truth is, I chose to stay for many reasons. I was not willing to abandon the kids or my mother. I stayed to be the buffer, to assure that they did not have to walk in my shoes. I stayed because they depended on me and so did she. I was their protector and caregiver. I had already lost my dignity and pride, had endured humiliation, and would never want to subject them to the same. I didn't eat food without permission for a long time because I was being obedient. I wanted to honor my mother just as the Bible told me to. I also had tried it in the beginning and the consequences were harsh. Not only was I not able to eat, the kids remained hungry too.

As far as telling someone, I did. I couldn't bring myself to tell it all, but I would tell the cops that she was isolating me from everyone and not letting me eat, but because my siblings said this was not true, they did not believe me. Not only that, I was not a quitter and after some time I had made peace with where I was. I trusted that there was a greater purpose.

Living through moments like these was sometimes unbearable, as I felt I was going to lose my mind or die from crying so hard. As a result of

that I built a safe place (imaginary) for myself where

no one could hurt me. I had found a way to separate

myself from the kicks, punches, and other abuse. I

would tap in and out of reality and my reality. It was

almost like my body would be being hit negatively

in this reality, but I would be playing dodge ball

somewhere else. I had created Tracy Land. Tracy

Land was a place where people saw me for who I

was. People saw me the way I was from a very

young age, which was a compassionate, sharing,

loving, and loyal person. A place where love lived

and hurt could not enter. I would bounce back to

reality sometimes and notice that, based on the look

on her face, it seemed like she wasn't going to stop

attacking me until I gave her the satisfaction she was

looking for. She wanted me to cry and scream in pain. When I would notice that I wasn't reacting normally I would let out a cry or wail so that she could finish.

I still have the ability to be physically present while being a million miles away mentally. In times of discomfort it has proven to be helpful for me. I am able to work under extreme pressure for long periods of time without feeling it the way I should. At times this has proven to be an issue, as I don't often know when to ask for help. Over the years this has contributed to a few emotional breakdowns. Just as I did when I was a kid and forgot to eat when it was safe, I forget to let people I know I need help sometimes until I am at my wits' end and in breakdown. It was survival as a child and habit now.

In reaching this point I was able to thrive while still being in this environment. I willed myself to live. Most of the pieces within this book took place between the ages of 12 and14. This time was all about learning to survive and be still. In order to survive I had to get creative. I have to say that even before this age, I was different than most of my peers in terms of my maturity and how in tune I was to the world around me. I cannot take credit for this, as I believe I was born this way. The rest was due to my faith. I believe that I survived these years the way I did because I was determined to. I was determined to be there for the babies, and a huge part of it was due to me wanting my mother's validation.

I observed my mother, studied her, and tried to understand why she behaved the way she did. I believe my mother's isolation damaged her. I believe that she was unhappy with her life, and as a result she made others unhappy. Accepting that I could not change this was also freeing to me, as I was able to focus on making sure I was okay. It took me a long time to figure this out, but once I did, I was okay.

I never stopped loving my mother, I just realized that she was incapable of receiving my love the way I expressed it, and she was also unable to love me the way I needed to be loved. I was about 13 ½ when I came to this realization.

Over the years I have also been asked "how did you do it?" People have wanted to know what sets me apart from others. The truth is, there is no one thing or one day that I can narrow down and say, "yeah that was it." I didn't have an epiphany one day. However, the only thing that sticks out is that I kept choosing to move forward. Positive self-talks, affirmations, and my faith were some of the methods I used. Looking back I could have run away, I chose not to. I could have told everything that was going on in my home, I chose not to. I could have eaten the food when I was told not to, however, I chose to obey. I could have refused to panhandle, grocery shop, and pay bills, but again I chose to obey. I could have jumped from that window and given up, but I CHOSE not to.

I was curious to see what living outside the box would feel like. I wanted to see how far I could go.

How many barriers I could break, and I did it all with invisible muscles built while being victimized. I was curious to see if I could have and be all the things that society said I couldn't. I did not like the attachments that came with being a victim. The stigma and low expectations attached to victims didn't sit well with me. I was crystal clear that I had been victimized, BUT I am no one's victim.

My life is a reflection of my choices. I also could work a 9 to 5, go home, cook dinner, and relax, but I choose to use my life to impact the lives of others. I choose to provoke change. I choose to use the stories of my past to encourage others. I choose to work in a field that keeps a part of me raw because the healing of others is that important to me. I choose to show up and work from my core because lives depend on it. I choose to be vulnerable so that those who have yet to get up know that it's possible. I choose to help those who care for others because I know what it's like to feel like giving up. I know what I needed when I was a child, teen, and adult, and I want to be that for others. My past was a setup for the healing of so many.

I have no regrets. I lived through the pieces shared and so many others and they all helped me become the person I am today. They are just a few stories from my childhood. I had many good days outside of this period of life. However, today I am the woman I am because of what I extracted from the trauma in my life. I wake up grateful for my life now, and that is only because I still remember life then. I understand the value of love and compassion and I aim to exude it.

I am one of many survivors of abuse and neglect. My survival and success in life is a testament to what perseverance and possibility looks like. I will continue to beat the odds. Fertilizer stinks and can seem unbearable, yet is a necessary part of the growth process. Who I am today is a result of the fertilizer I rose from. I always say, "You cannot run through a burning building and expect not to come out smelling like smoke." I choose to focus on the fact that I survived the burning building while helping to free others who may be stuck on the stench their journey left on them. I am here to help them see that we survived.

Over the years after sharing one or two pieces of my life with others, the usual responses have been that "I would never have known or guessed this happened to you," and "you don't look like what you have been through." My thoughts regarding this matter have always been; *what am I supposed to look like? of course I don't and that's exactly why I pushed past barriers.* I refused to look like a wounded puppy and I don't want to be treated based on what happened to me (as a victim). I am a good example and sample of what is possible when you are determined and persevere. I want youth who have experienced trauma to have a good path to follow. I want for those who work with trauma victims to see them beyond their wounds and look for the possibilities. I believe it's time to give trauma a facelift, as we often remain stuck on what happened, as opposed to what can be produced as a result of trauma. Long faces and sad stories left alone, only impregnate a victim with more trauma. Let us choose to identify strengths and recognize resilience so that triumph can begin to impregnate individuals with possibility.

Heart Aspirations

Tracy Young, M.S.W.

Speaker | Trainer | Consultant | Coach

Website: *http://www.heartaspirations.org*

Email: *tracy@heartaspirations.org*

http://www.facebook.com/heartaspirations

http://www.instagram.com/heartaspirations

YouTube *http://www.youtube.com/heartaspirations*

*9 7 8 1 9 4 8 7 7 7 1 0 0 *